HAPPY EASTER
Color By Numbers For Kids

This Book Belongs To

....

TEST YOUR COLOR HERE

1.Orangey Yellow 2.Orange 3.Aqua Green
4.Trendy Pink 5.Pastel Grey 6.White
7.Woodrush 8.Light Rose 9.Dark Salmon

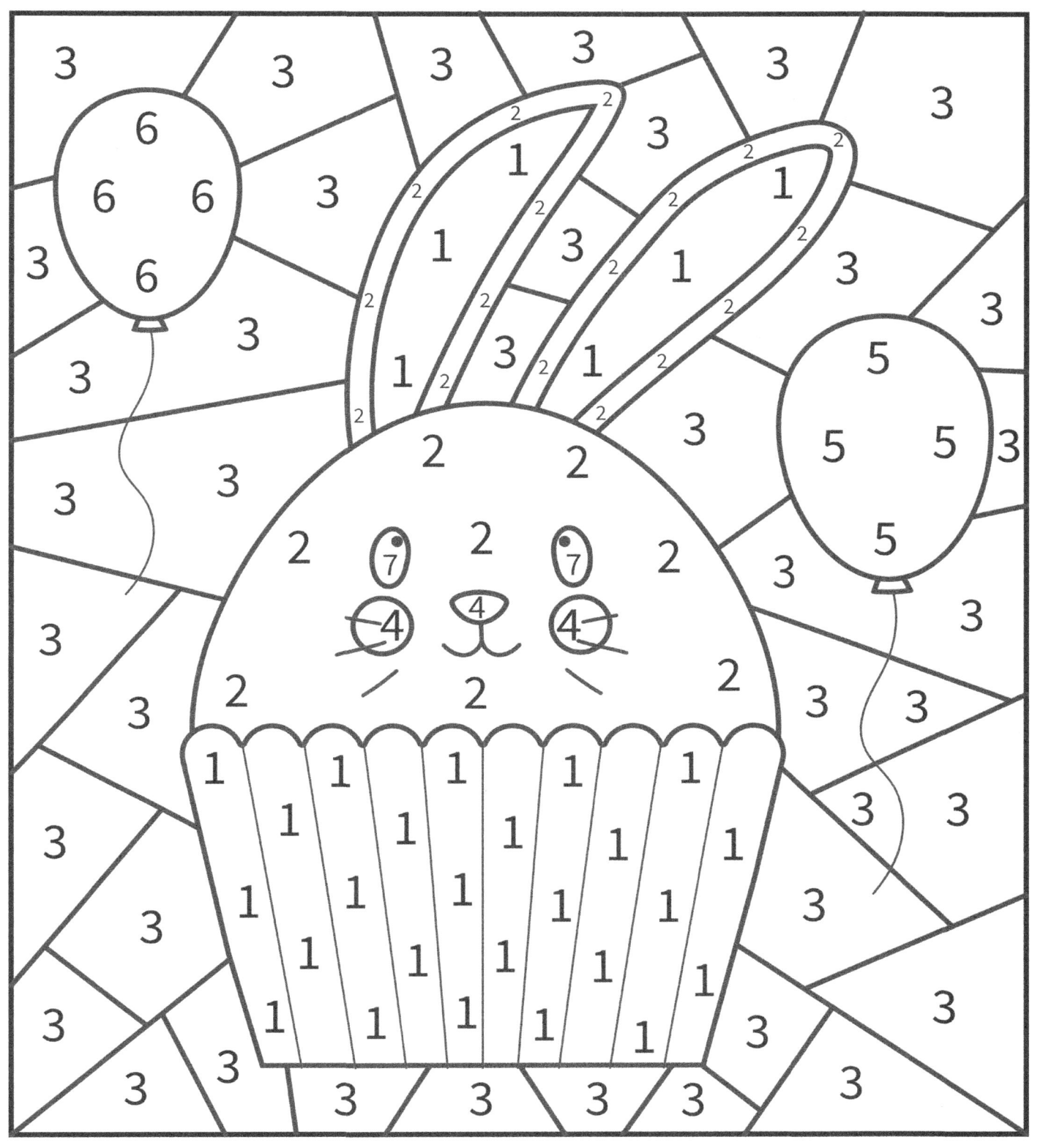

1.Sweet Pink 2.White 3.Flat Green 4.Dull Purple
5.Light Purple 6.Pastel Orange 7.Copper Rust

1.Light Sea Green 2.Deep Teal 3.Mango Orange
4.Colonial White 5.Saffron Mango 6.Light Orange
7.Coral Pink 8.Black 9.Watermelon Pink

1.Deep Lilac 2.Golden 3.Sienna 4.Sandy Beach
5.Watermelon 6.Heavy Metal 7.Cerulean

1.Dawn Pink 2.White 3.Warm Purple
4.Egg Blue 5.Light Pink 6.Rose Pink
7.Redwood 8.Goldenrod 9.Green Teal

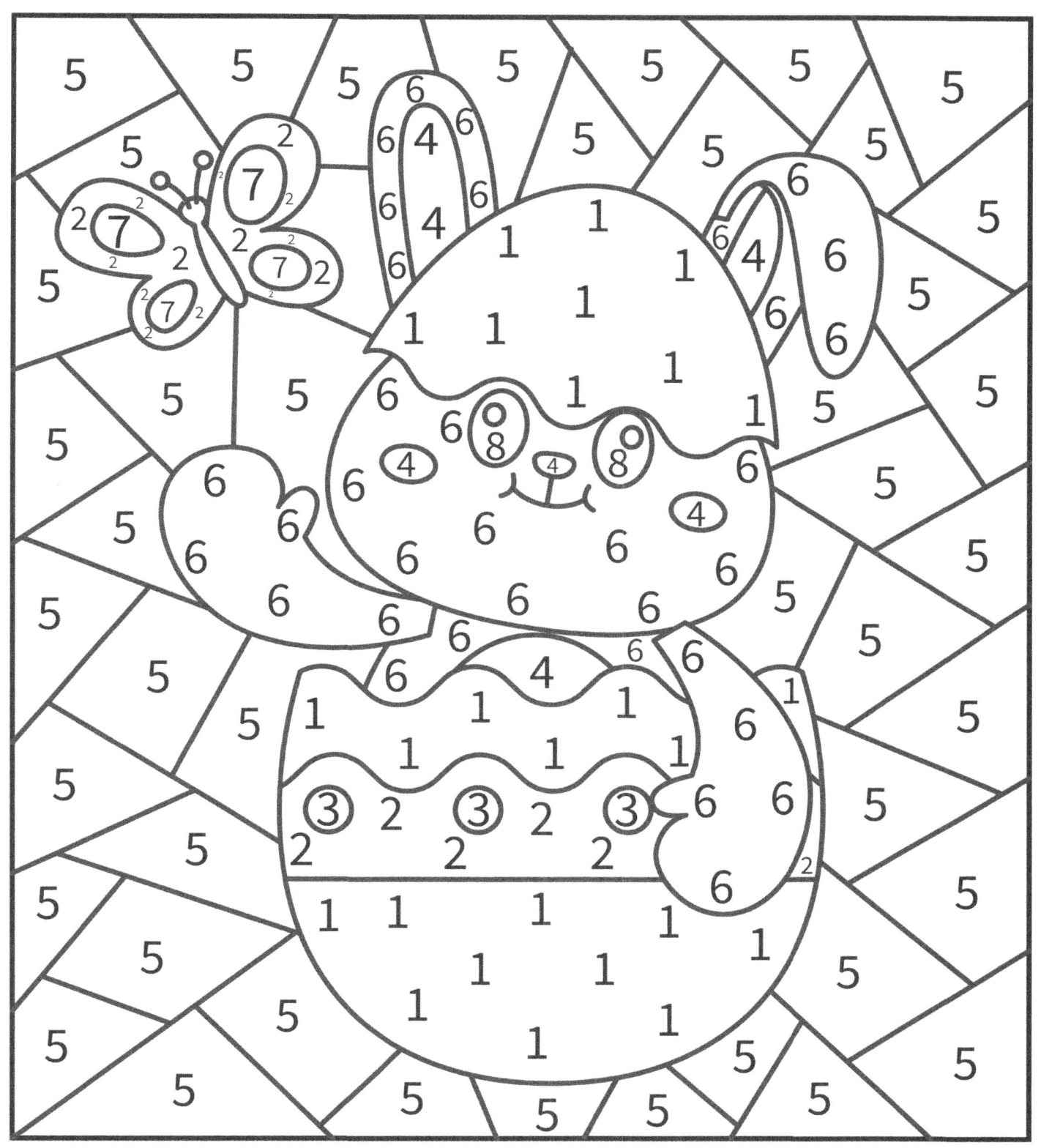

1.Dark Blue 2.Orange 3.Light Gold 4.Watermelon
5.Bright Cerulean 6.White 7.Yellow 8.Black

1.Rose Pink 2.Light Gold 3.White 4.Pastel Orange
5.Dull Purple 6.Fountain Blue

1.Soft Pink 2.Watermelon 3.Soft Blue 4.White
5.Pale Pink 6.Green Teal

1.Butterfly Blue 2.Light Rose 3.Golden Glow
4.Lights Blue 5.Sunrise Orange 6.Orangey Yellow
7.White 8.Woodrush

1.Sweet Pink 2.Light Orange 3.Water Leaf
4.Watermelon 5.White 6.Golden 7.Green Onion

1.Teal Blue 2.Bright Cerulean 3.Bright Gold
4.Light Eggplant 5.Sienna 6.White
7.Heavy Metal 8.Pink

1.Faded Orange 2.White 3.Light Coral
4.Yellow 5.Dark Coral 6.Butterfly Blue

1.Peppermint 2.Salmon Pink 3.Dawn Pink
4.Dark Salmon 5.Brown Sugar 6.White
7.Green 8.Dark

1.Pearl Aqua 2.Dark Salmon 3.Flame Pea
4.Tea Rose 5.Light Pink 6.Dark Pink
7.Cerulean 8.Pinkish Red

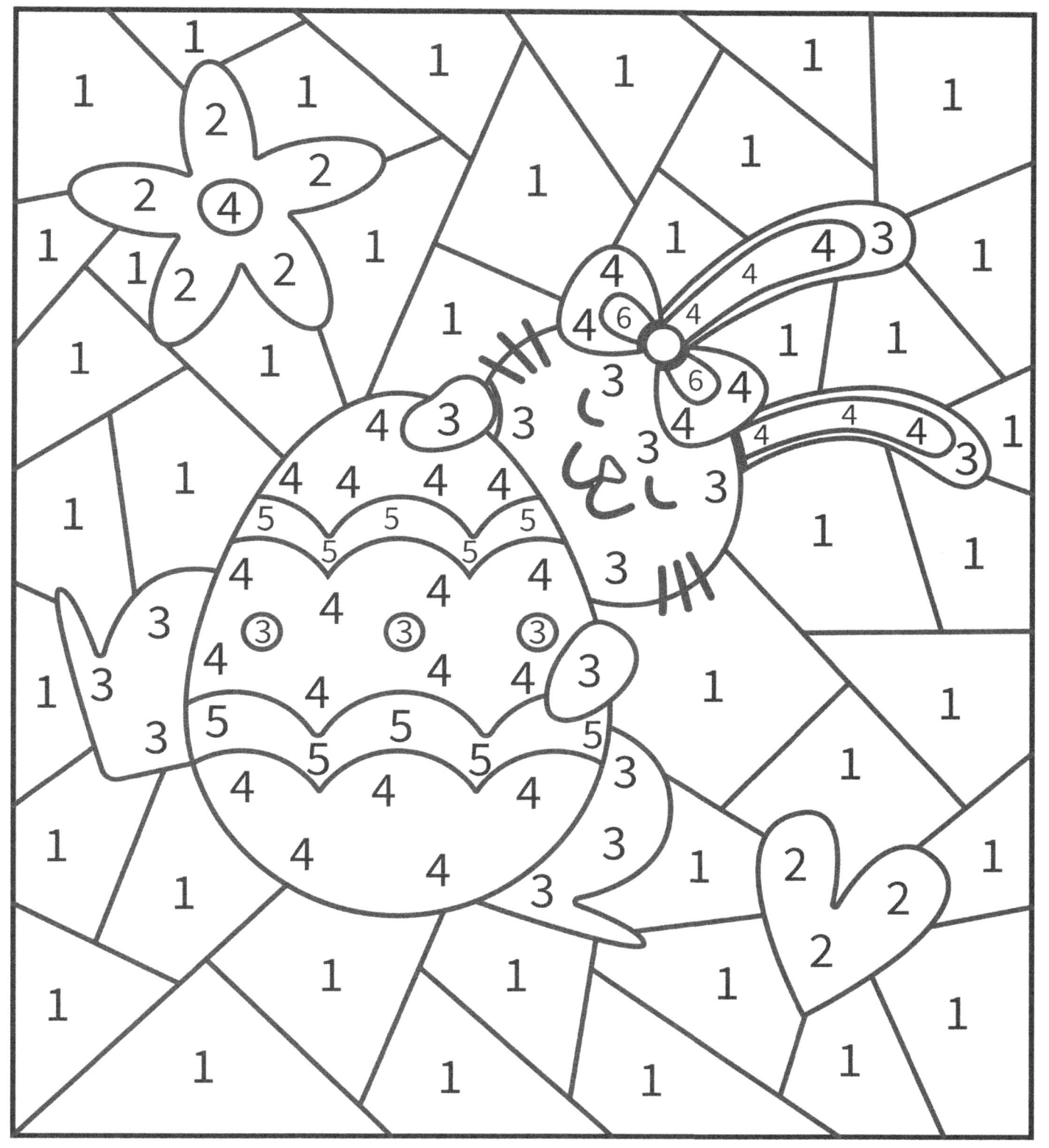

1.Green Onion 2.Peachy Pink 3.White
4.Rose Pink 5.Corn Yellow 6.Deep Blush

1.Light Gold 2.Rose Pink 3.White
4.Deep Blush 5.Bright Cerulean

1.White 2.Sweet Pink 3.Pale Pink
4.Green Onion

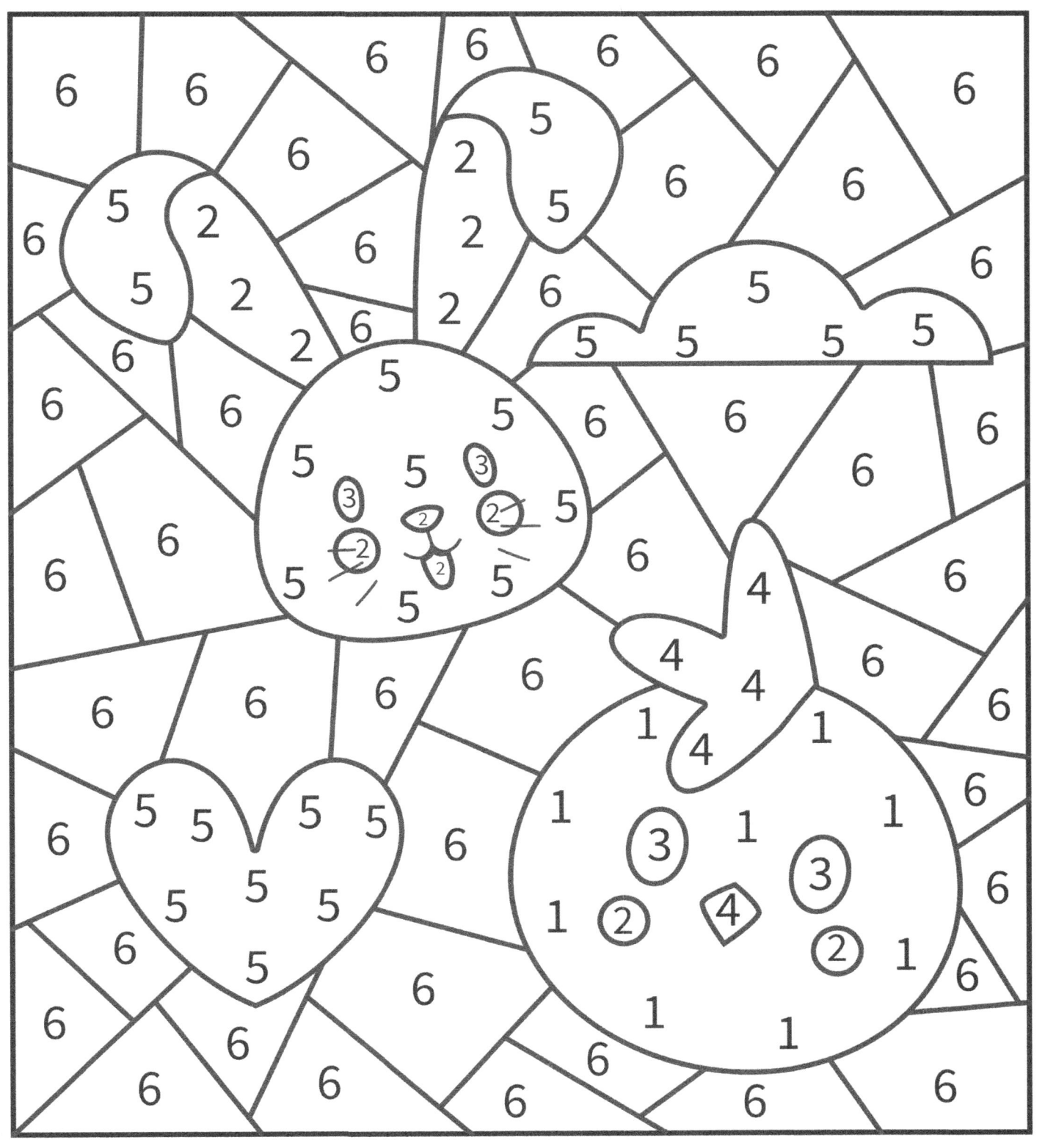

1.Light Gold 2.Sweet Pink 3.Dull Purple
4.Dark Orange 5.White 6.Lily

1.Deep Lilac 2.Deep Peach 3.Pale Salmon
4.Light Coral 5.Cocoa Bean 6.Aqua Marine

1. White 2.Pink Lace 3.Light Rose 4.Dull Yellow
5.Fountain Blue

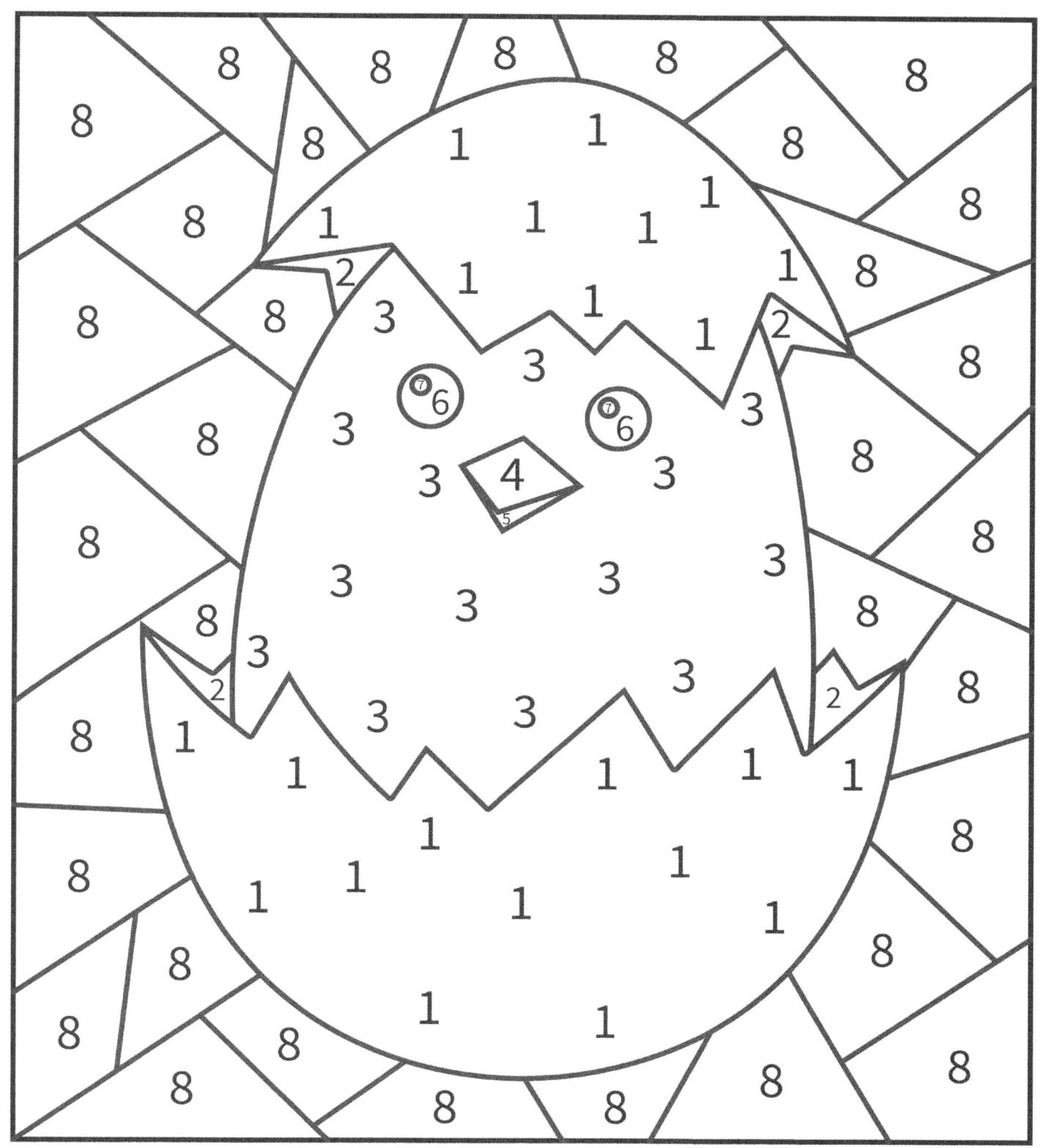

1.Geyser 2.Light Blue 3.Light Mustard
4.Mango Orange 5.Tomato 6.Bright Grey
7.White 8.Light Olive

1.Colonial White 2.Coral Pink 3.Melon
4.Pale Salmon 5.Grey Teal 6.Black

1.Dark Salmon 2.Golden Brown 3.Pastel Red
4.White 5.Sunrise Orange 6.Redwood

1.Classic Rose 2.Sienna 3.Yellow 4.Blue
5.Candy Pink 6.White 7.Orange Gold

1.White 2.Blue Green 3.Light Gold 4.Fountain Blue
5.Pastel Orange 6.Rosy Pink 7.Grey Pink

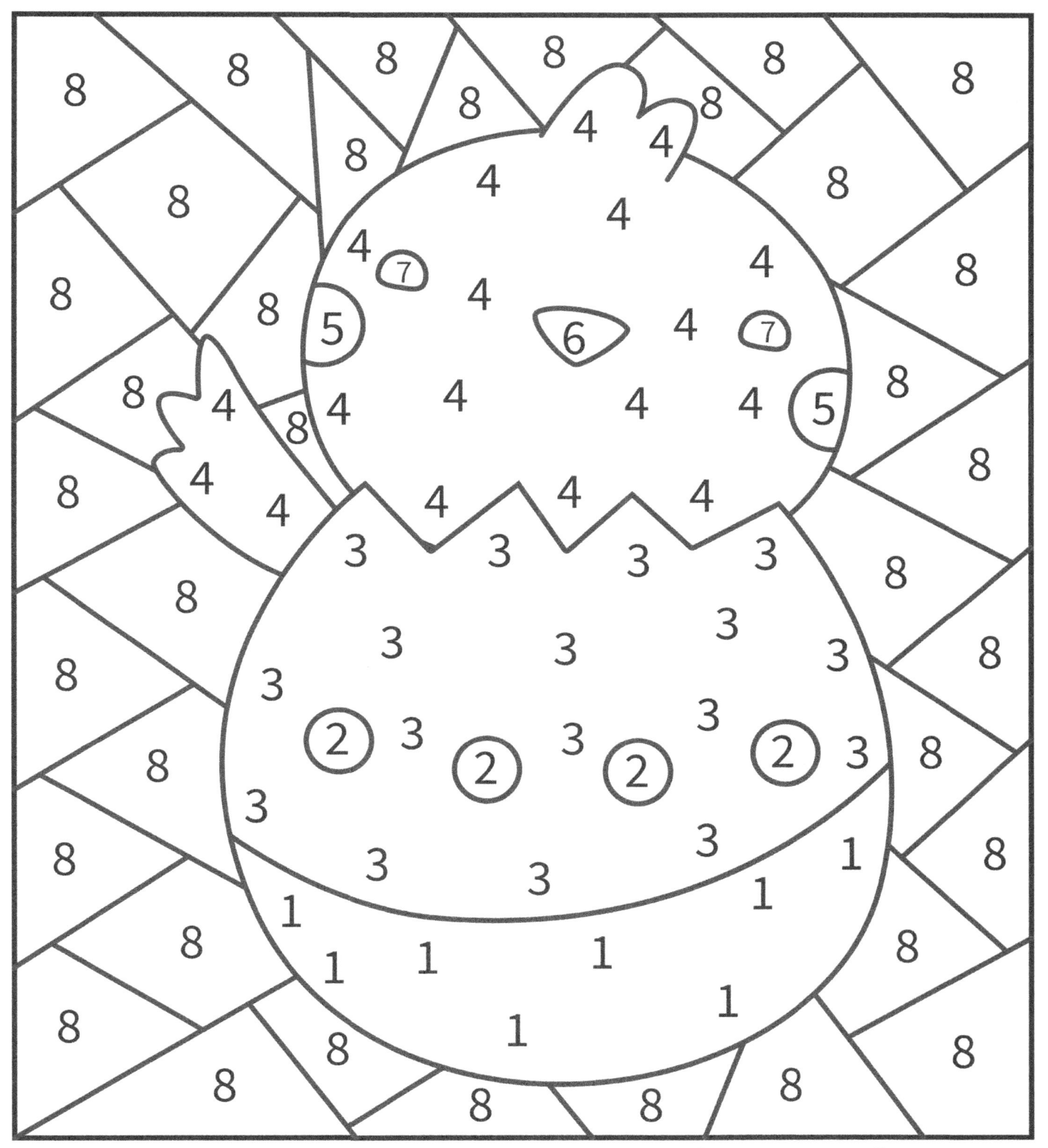

1.Dull Pink 2.Turquoise Blue 3.White
4.Light Gold 5.Rosy Pink 6.Deep Saffron
7.Grape Purple 8.Dull Green

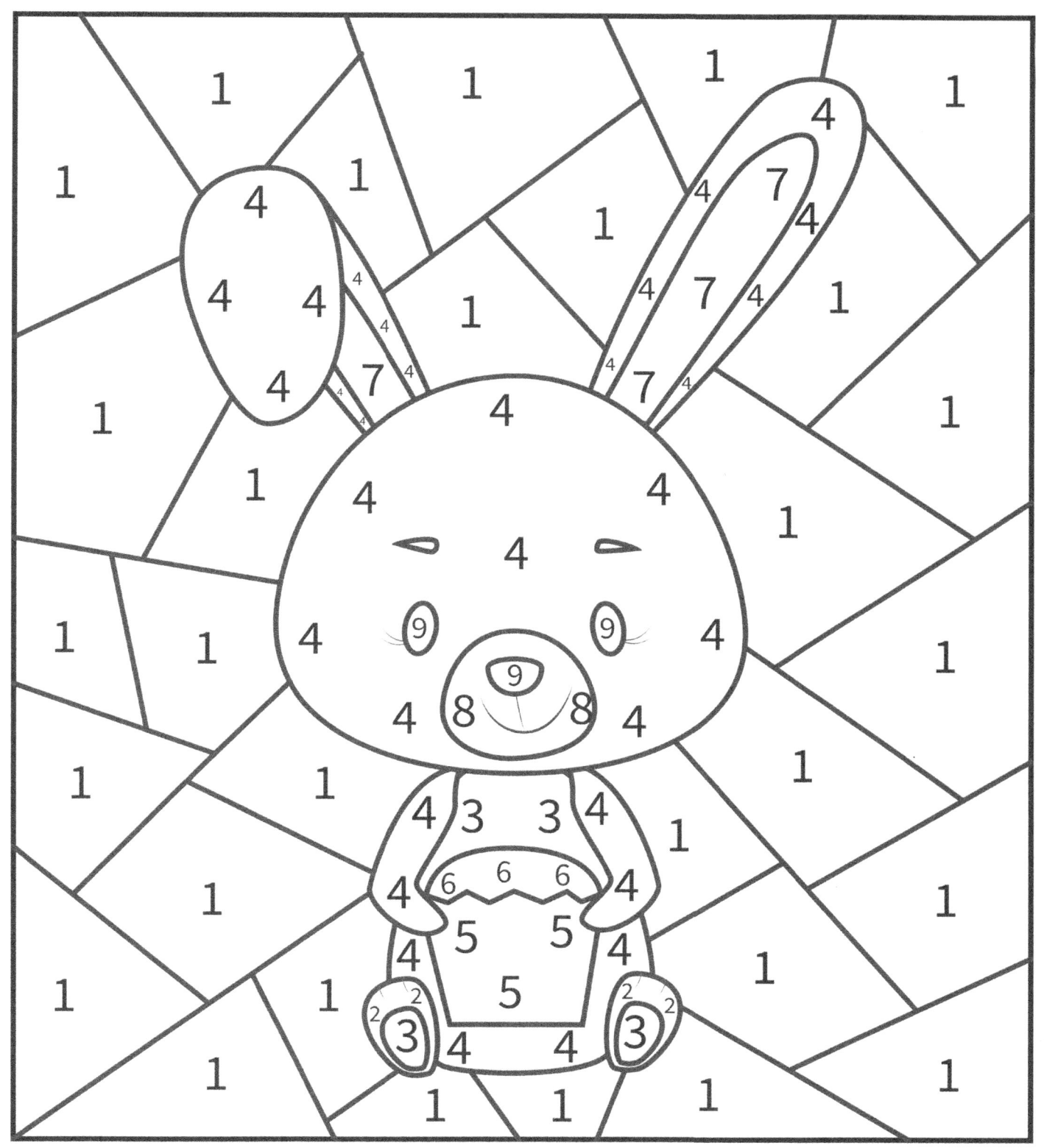

1.Dull Orange 2.Jeans Blue 3.Coral Blue
4.Light Blue 5.Light Green 6.Burly Wood
7.Pink Rose 8.Frosted Mint 9.Black

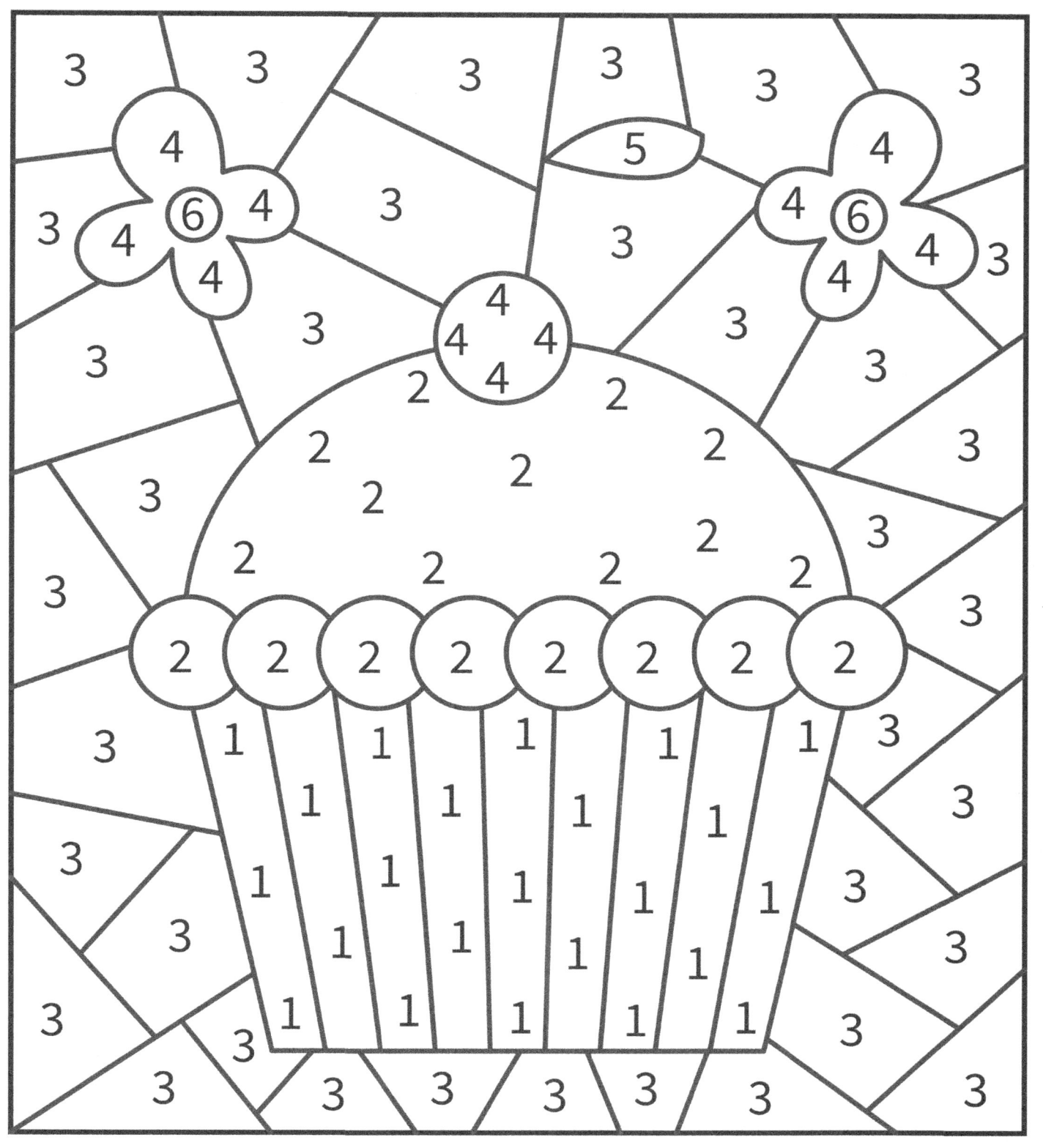

1.Golden 2.Burnt Red 3.Light Olive
4.Light Red 5.Grey Teal 6.White

1.Cerulean Blue 2.Rich Blue 3.Light Orchid
4.Golden 5.White 6.Burnt Red 7.Watermelon

1.White 2.Light Olive 3.Cloudy Blue 4.Watermelon
5.Mandys Pink 6.Black 7.Rust Red

1.Wheatfield 2.Light Salmon 3.Deep Coffee
4.Dull Blue

1.Coral Pink 2.Wheatfield 3.Lights Blue
4.Sap Green

1.Saffron Mango 2.Woody Brown 3.Dawn Pink
4.Sap Green

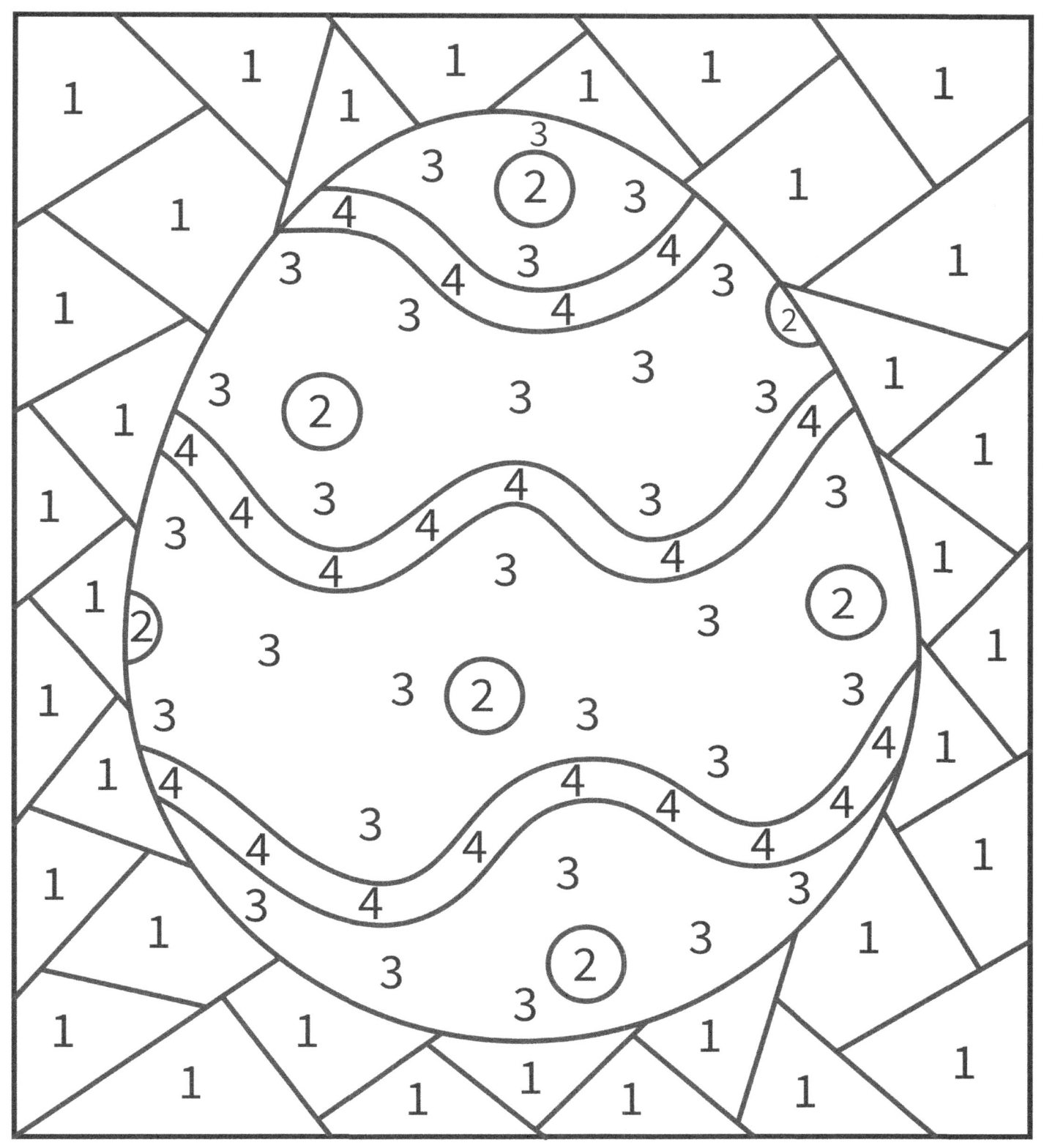

1.Topaz 2.Red Pink 3.Sunglow 4.Deep Saffron

1.Deep Peach 2.Peach Yellow 3.Peanut
4.Papaya Whip 5.Coral Pink 6.Blue Bell

1.Pale Rose 2.Linen 3.Pink 4.White
5.Charcoal Grey 6.Fountain Blue

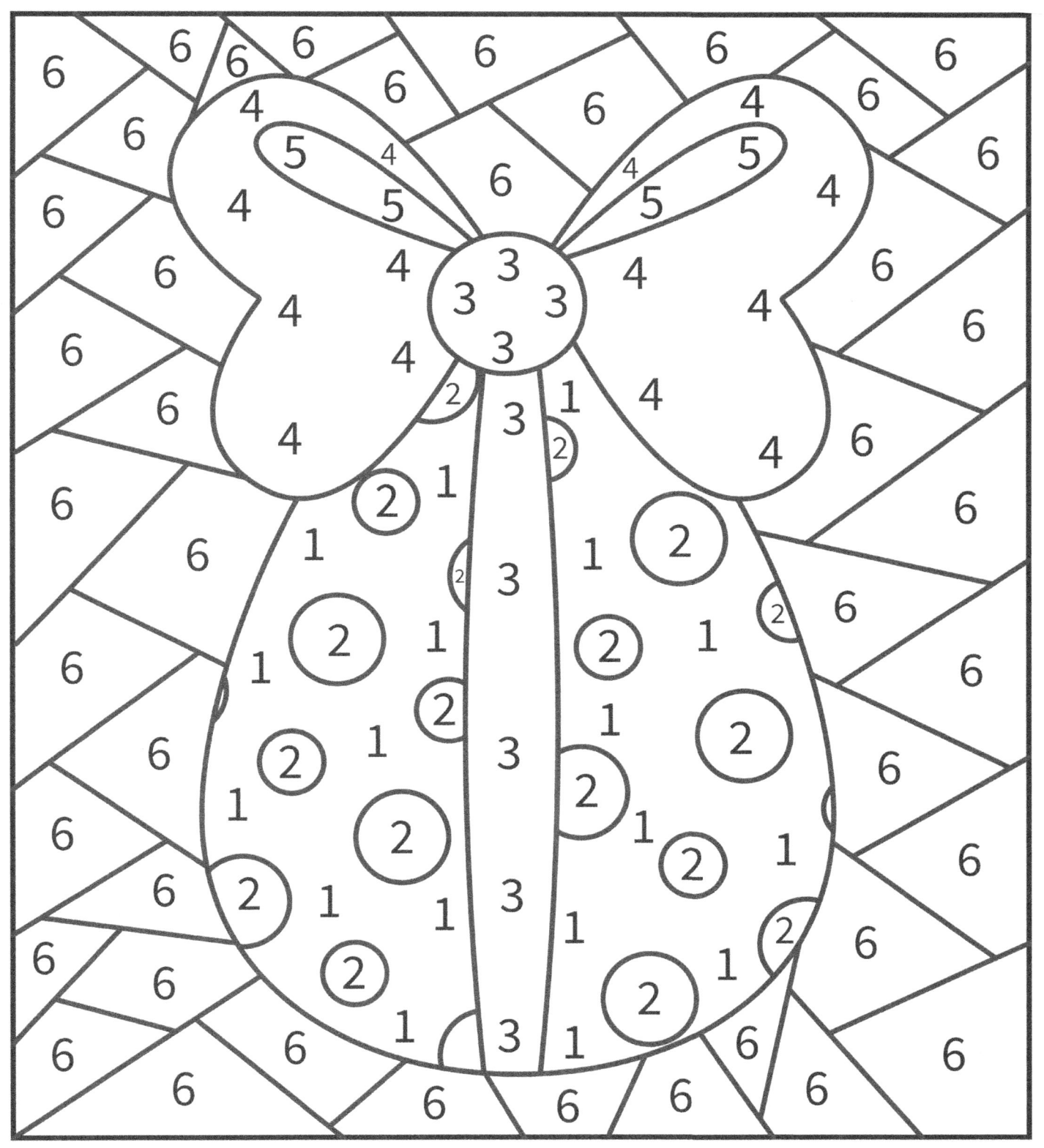

1.Cumin 2.Cavern Pink 3.Light Orange
4.Carrot Orange 5.Papaya Orange 6.Blue Bell

1.Melon 2.Almond 3.Dawn Pink 4.Light Orchid
5.Peanut 6.Coral Pink 7.Fountain Blue

1.Dark Orchid 2.Deep Coffee 3.Copper Rose
4.Red 5.Fountain Blue

1.Purplish Pink 2.Deep Lilac 3.White
4.Light Rose 5.Peach 6.Cerulean 7.Coffee

Made in United States
Orlando, FL
13 April 2024

45773985R10046